where the night sings

Faith Atuhumuze

edited by Shirley Bell

THE
BLUE
NIB

where the night sings

First published in Great Britain in 2018 by The Blue Nib

ISBN 978-1999955007

For Brenda Asiimwe

CONTENTS

soapbox disciple

i'm a textbook believer-
healed by the god of the indeterminate day

i.
it's january and my brother counts his blessings
in beads of sweat wetting the ground he cultivates as
an altar
he waters his god 'til his bones squeak like rusted
trains
                              'til we're run out of drums playing
our stomachs

ii.
in the kitchen, my sister feeds pages of a hymnal
onto a wood fire between full mouth blows
her singing voice is an attic for smoke
when she says she loves me- still-
it's a voice of god breaking
through the rain stuck in her throat

iii.

at the dining table

we shift from sat-in sides

of our half eaten platter-

there, i believe in the god my mother ties

on the corner of her wrapper

you'll have to undress her to see the wounds

healing on her knees; she wears scabs

as enemy deaths peeling off her walls of war

she laughs like a woman giving birth

and there is something that hurts;

hurts worse than soaped eyes

she rinses with wordless devotions-

hurts worse than laughter in a foreign tongue

'pray, my child, pray'

she unhooks my hands from the clutch on my belly,

turns them palm up to heaven, weighing them on the

scales in her eyes and finding them not enough to

hold the sea to put out the hell burning up my legs

'pray, my child, pray'

iv.

i inherit the god of my father

the afternoon we sit under a jack-fruit tree

drawing banana beer from a calabash

lapping between a red mane sky

and papaya-sapped mouths,

our silence confirms love's vocation

when he speaks, it's as pockets being emptied

his teeth clatter like house keys pulling threads

from his belly, transparency burns through his words

it almost hurts looking him in the eye,

every night i close mine in sleep

i hear his voice as lint filling up the tears in me

v.

in december, the weather is wet

i'm striking matches upon my fingers

to heat my room

when i find the wooden god
my grandmother left behind my door in july

i set fire to his hands and watch her god burn

through himself to save me

i'm thinking he doesn't wear death too well

when i wipe down his ashen throne

for the god of the next person to *(pretend to)* love me

if not for the relentless drought

we wouldn't have sought out

things that hold water

othered

there is a girl at every corner stop

with a precarious border wedged between her legs

petting an eight month barrenness held

together by a starched cotton belt

she sneezes through a closed fist

begging for someone with enough

courage to treat her as human

her breasts peer through a threadbare blouse

just as a sun starting to appear through the mist

so much fullness spills from places of emptiness

a girl fallen in love with impermanence

she pets the goat hour

than the hollow side of her bed

there's a grieving aunt on her bedroom floor

whose dirge found the cracks in the wall

'you've killed me!'-

the unhurried death of unpaid bride price

for a girl whose hymen

is still wearing off the man who

hid her beneath his bed

while cannon mouths kissed the other side of the wall

the father who denied her his name

cradled the gun 'til they fell, both

at the mouth of a barrel

the same voiceless hour of the genocide

she found her sister's body in the yard

wilting beneath a rose bush

she, too, naked and without a name.

she never knew poetry;

her kind of death died with her

the uncle who took her mother's hand

took along what was left of her father's land

from burying faceless heirs and saints

she didn't show up for the funerals
the night she crossed the Kagera
with a firm grip on the coarse hands of strangers
she now called brother

it was not a religious thing
when they went three days on water
and the stones would skin their feet
before the devil made offers for bread

the war had grown to the kind of might
only reserved for God

the journey was fatiguing as
much as it was freeing
it tightened her calves and
blacked her heels
the suffering both hardening
and disbanding her of grace
it only left fear;
the fear to go back when there was nowhere to go
back to

the fear to say goodbye when there was no one to say

goodbye to

cloaked in mortality statistics

she wears the dead-

bodies of her lost clan

her father, upon her chest,

giving up the fight

to stay contained

a sister that never learned to say yes

to vulnerability, inside her womb

a mother upon shoulders parting

from her heart each time

she lifted her hands to pray

'don't leave me'

every night she bathes in the river,

she watches them fall

through her hands all over again

and there still stands, by the city on the hill,

a David, winking through the rear-sight of a rifle

he left his god on his nightstand

and the war was not,

in its raucous boastings

but in the silence that lingered

there is a girl at every corner stop

a branded whore,

with prepositions at her doorstep

they come at her with trivial features

Tom with a volcano of lies

Adam, a seasonal river, here today

gone the next

then there is Sam with a tattoo on her thigh

thinning in the thick of things-

all seek to leave

precarious borders between her legs

if it weren't for the scabs

i wouldn't know how thick skin can be,

in broken places

corrosive

i believe every woman should, at least once, smoke a
cigarette
and when between bouts of cough, she passes it to
the moment
watch- how the hour spits back pollution to the wind
without nursing it between its lungs.

and when the sun blisters the night sky, know,
to reach for a rub of alcohol

my mother nursed all her infants
in the shadow of a shrub
her legs, straddling a garden hoe
her breast would run out of milk but never faith

i believe every child should be taken to a church when
they're teething
and when the stained glass flashes its blush at them
learn that no amount of beauty can stop
shit that's ready to come out

and when the priest nudges his garb to symmetry
yet no matter what angle he curves his tongue

his vernacular finds a busted seam to spill through,
learn,
that the math might not always add up

i learned from my mother to
in no way rush my expectations.

i always found ways to admire her hope
at five,
with hair wanting out of the bantu knots
a rip dragging itself across her dress
and cracks digging up her heels,
she bent
teaching us to lace our shoes into bunny ears

but children that age should be taught how to fall
over their own feet and how to get up
not how to tie corpses to their feet
no one should learn vulnerability when they're so
damn young

at eighteen, you'd compare skinned knees
to the times you prayed

or was it 'played'
when you folded scripture into paper kites
because your father could never afford a kite
and the black and white bible reminded you
you'll always be words but never the page
you held onto the string
'til the kite was lost to the uncertainty of clouds
and your hand was bleeding
the time heaven bartered your laughter for war

you steep your anger in metaphor
and the automated bullshit that rhymes
only to wake up one day with the reputation of a bad
poet
but you can only stop scratching when you stop
itching
so you promise
this is going somewhere

only a film of dust to show

for the stretch of desert we walked

pain never learned to hold on

wandering jew

if you give me the right price
i'll loosen my happiness
from the tether on my undergarments
and give it to you

if you sit me at the right
edge of darkness
wipe the crescent smile
off the night sky
i'll tear you love-
songs into suicide notes

i wouldn't be a poet
if i had a mind for lovers
who hold my head to the cradle
of their stillborn- my mouth,
blowing
quick fixes for blank profanities

my third finger learned to sore

grasping for wandering jew

in our untamed garden

my hands were weaving fiber dolls

when all little girls learned

to paint their faces in chalk

there are nights i face

away from the moon

pretending it's a halo

pretending not to hear angels laugh

the morning i spend at FACO

sandpaper jerking-

off my skin

i'll burn through my body-

ask 'is that incense

enough to climb

down a god from a high horse

i was too poor to ride?'

there are times when prayers

come at me as suitors

crawling debased hands

up my upturned chest

they rise as anthems

i say- sing them

until they're all dried out of lament

i say- sing them

until all my flags are dropped to half-mast

i lace my fingers into ropes to

tether piquant grace

to my bed stand

'til she's fair in web and dust

'til she learns not

to wear silent words to fist fights

i keep open

the doors to war

since my first wound healed

like a whirlwind

scaled off- like it was never there

whooshing by the overhang rubbish

of my identity

that crawls through my skin

in spastic jerks

i close my eyes,

let static make love to me

'til i'm all rained out

i write smug masochism

into verse 'til my fingers

start to build defenses

but women like me

are built

for gallantry

the holes between our legs

bury victims

our monthly bleeding

is an exorcism

of our crowded graveyards

these hands are shovels-
palms so cracked
i wonder how they lift up worship
without wringing it out
how they contain dreams
without leaving peepholes

they take the proverbial feather from a hat
and repeat the line over and over
'is that enough for a blanket?'
they ask before they start all over again

they'll trade twenty-year closures
for handouts
and sin is a desert thorn
filling up the space
at a funeral of flowers

a lot's been given up on
beauty behind a rusted doorknob
weeds growing atop a grass thatch

love hidden between clandestine metaphors

but what do i know about destruction or
love?

o man of wanting, lay your claim
pause your pending chapter
i'll undo my wrapper
if you come at me
with good intentions
and maybe you, too,
against the backdrop of gilded disposition,
will be laid
down

strumming a hymn

fingers pluck- string to string

in between, an emptiness

remember love

remember the kink in our native tongue
that fermented days of wanting
'til we were ripe and fizzing
at eighteen
when we had nothing,
not pride on our plate
to feed our hunger

we sat our backs sore
discussing religion
unapologetic for our hands
that loved with no room for begging
remember how we wondered
if we loved like Christ

flowers were out of season
and we had miles to walk

we were stuck inside a love song
our bodies holding down a thirst
between foot sores and a falling sweat

but we came
and we loved

but didn't hold on

our chests have since filled out
our pockets run out of room for sunshine
and the straws we pulled
have left a host of wildflowers

now we're barely here
bumbling through similes
to define our loving
as patients needling water through veins
as birds picking song off morning branches
as in... like... as in... love

i jostle for white space
where you
pry into ashtrays
for the discarded odes
of nasal singing whores

there are days that seem so large they blur

yet here we are, the faintest of things, fading in-

a blink, an itch that won't quit

curious graces

there's a gif stuck at our turning of pages

a static, at our crossing of paths

waiting-

it begins as a pastoral fiddle surging through barren

anthills

waiting-

it thins as the poise of a thorn surging between petals

we, smile toothless-

the little windows in our poverty

through which our curious graces peer

the church prays in bare sighs

that break its lamentations

into smaller, marketable hallelujahs

the cracks grow weeds

that whore out their flowers

to passing cars

and funerals wear the color of our skin

but we swear your name as collateral

all these years, we still haven't learned the rules of

concession.

the pot that once fetched our drink

has become a host of webs.

the shard that once cut our hair

is now breaking our neck

but it's amazing how still,

like a child to a stranger on the bus,

we smile, wet and over another's back

locusts have sheared our overgrown hope-

our fond white memories slowly ghosted

on the edge of our cigarette,

amazing how, still,

love gets around more than suicide notes

turn your bed to the window

draw the curtains

let the sun fill the dents in your pillow

this barren expanse

speak of the sun-tanned plate hiding its freckles

in the skirts of a night sky

where she dwarfs a litter of stars

the poets worship her glow

tonight, she wears a soft yellow

of the flag planting its feet

in the cheeks of my home

she's face-up and empty

as the plate placed before me

we- are both barren

she, recollects the stars that fell through her toes

and i, the children i buried in plastic bags

i, refuse to open my mouth when they ask me to

speak

because i refuse to cry my dehydration to the grave

i layer unspoken words

to cushion my otherwise hollow belly

so they won't hear me rattle

when the wind blows through my holes

that would rather let love go

yes, i hold lovers between my teeth

and refuse to spit when they fold

me at the corner, pin me to cardboard

walls, eye me once over and leave this poster

child of poverty to fade in their hail

the poets worship the moon's glow tonight

from where i stand, she wears pain

and i

want none of it

when we were younger

we kicked stones along the path
saying,

'i was here and i took, with me, all that i could'

a little ways down-

'i was here, i left a mark- a pebble, a foundation'

now we're older

we lift our feet

afraid to raise the dust

'come home' mother says to me

i.

my breath hazes up the glass window, i reach out a
mindless finger to trace my shadow wishing myself to
disappear too when the light does. i am going to the
city of light, as clouds do, sigh after next. and birds.
and all things that have breath.

i, am a woman searching for salvation.

my hand grips the shame of a putout splinter into the
buckle of a seat that offers no guarantees, feeling my
skin mesh guilt-like-sin over me when *he* casts my
name off *his* tongue like disease-

home is the trail of desert dwarfing south into a biblical
obscurity

i count miles to my father's threshold to sleep
careful to plant my bubble gum feet into the ground
i walk, afraid *they'll* see   my tremble
an earthquake still warps through my rift valley village

they ask me where i'm from

i-

am Hemingway's failed experiment

come from a Paris underground

where i left everything i had seen

behind the last turnstile,

unheard all its romances

except the creak of the train that carried me back

i come from the bending

branches of a willow

that drank out of la seine

where lovers loved

while she taught me how to weep

ii.

'come home' mother says to me

iii.

'i am going to the city of love'

as dreamers do, kip after next

i tell mother

i met a western man

at the St. Michel stop he called

me 'jolie'

but this i do not tell her

how he wore my hair upon his hand

called *this* tribal

how i combed out my knots

sat up whole nights

gluing Brazilian weaves to my scalp

and how, even then,

he didn't find my beautiful beautiful

i home with the masochists

trading lonely for the courage of a thong

wedging up my unborn infants

a drought burns between my legs
a drought burns down my father's garden
like all seeds, we both could use a rain

iv.
mother walks me to the threshold and asks what i see.
i have not been home for years and i see
nothing. *'pretend you're in labor and look again'* she says
ever so patiently.

and i, have been labored.

so i see her. and how much more i've looked like her
since my last visit. a couple wrinkles converge at the
fire burning in her eyes when she smiles. i recognize
them with vivid familiarity. empathy warming her stiff
hands, endurance with a leg thrown over the other
and a peace that hymns when she blinks.

i see her. and how much less i've looked like her since
my last visit. my own face is starting to crease, it folds
into itself like gullies- running off the grin of a
missing-tooth-day, the blink in the eye that believed in
god, the lisp on the tongue that wet through words
until they were too heavy to speak i swallowed them. i
notice the papyrus thatch, that taught me how to
stutter when it hushed rain songs into whisper, is
gone and home is an aluminum blinding that chokes
back prayers. mother asks me what i see- where the
roof throws up a sun back to god before it touches
my feet.

the rock on which i stumbled has pebbled into the
grass   on which i played has tamed
a garden of weeds   whose ears i plucked has
learned to flower   and i, am a ridging of gravel
and brown sand still learning   to still

mother is making pound in a wooden mortar when
she tells me Ruth got married- we went to school
together. she pretends the peanuts are the man that
broke my heart and pestles them to dust cussing
through the shadow of the bang, bang - 'the devil will
be shamed'- she prays before we reach for what she
serves with bare hands.

and home is the reed mat on the kitchen floor where we sit,
silent mouths reiterating through yesterdays

hope is as a wallflower

one day pulling down the sun from the sky

the next, standing out a dance

propped against our made-up walls

the woman on the wall needs a patting [mirrors]

i.
we are narcissists
breaking in a new mirror
from the look of our faces

we'll stand anything in her front
and want it to look like us;….
asking it to be full enough,
fair enough,
good enough.

we are animated,
replicating trials to feed our fancy.
she won't reflect our emptiness

she sits like a lady,
her back against the wall,
stilling a shiver until obligated to speak

and that takes a hammer. a shaking. an open barrel.

ii.
no one looks at the mirror.

she wears a coat of dust and man(s)
a fading wall, unblinking to a room full
of light while we change our face;

she clenches a tear between her
teeth as tweezers yank all her
ha(e)irs
off her brow; another, as mascara sticks beat
her eyes into obedience. 'crying is for the feeble,'
she chants as we test vacant smiles
on a full set of teeth.

we leave her to watch the walls.
she doesn't ask to go with us and
we don't ask.

she knows all of our washable faces
she knows the pulse of the heart of a wall.

iii.
we fold our paper hearts into kites and float them away
afraid to be interpreted by an obscure woman that never tests
her wisdom anywhere. we purse our prayers beneath lipstick
pu(a)cks afraid she'll find the wrong version of god.

she mourns herself to sleep,
dreams herself awake- on nights
when we walk into the bathroom
with lights off. the woman on the wall
listens to our passive silences-
she folds at the top, like church windows-
endless, like she could go on forever-
into walls. we choose to drain our tears face down

iv.
she pales in powdered sentiments,
wears our acne like graveyards that refuse death to be final,
we keep coming back, patting down our pretenses
until we are a canvas of scars

she asks *'what life do you search for inside this dying?'*

v.
we automate our humdrum
as she fills up her blank spaces with everything
a lifting comb, a spray can, a wounded mouth,
an unmade bed, a wall
and at the extreme end, a window-
that goes nowhere

we automate until we are full of ourselves.
until what we see is more tangible than our real selves

she smells our pretenses
and fights us; like women do-holding
her tongue between her teeth

she looks at us. hard.
until we can see our selves inside her eyes.
nailed down, spat on, sprayed on-
buoyant, in a coat of dust

we see our silvered hearts inside a glass cage
that, like all other things, break

but that takes a hammer. a shaking. an open barrel.

the day I was taught to spell-out my
name

is the day i lost myself

        inside creeds and alphabets

you kill the light that doesn't sing for you

our headlamps cut through wrists of night
leaving scars that we're too mortal to acknowledge

we walk blind into stairs,
misplaced shoes,
wall-
into each other

'neath our feet, concrete floors murmur
an eagerness for the fray

i am a firefly wandered
into narcissus' bedstead

i revere your witchcraft
clap my wings to sing you songs
'cause we are young
 and everything is careless
 and we whore out our hearts like food stamps

'cause we are young
 and everything is important
we listen with the keenness of deities
watch with the quickness of predators

i see you sit on the hands of your pretences
with the sobering clarity of 3am
when you throw me out in paper-
bags, i'm sure to thaw

the moon sheds its dust to a knob
and that's the star i follow, cracked,
back the road that led me to you

there is morning breaking through my legs
but you still play
in the puddle of our skidding
still hold shallow rain of our marlboro halos

the night fingers her fiddle

a bottle of gin running low

a crap lined window- ten pigeons long

everything pulls down the drapes

yowanina

i.

at thirteen, her chest is starting to swell
with every word she would yet learn to speak.
the rosary sinks inside the ridge
digging between her rib-
cage; her aunts are getting infatuated
with the idea of cows, they
poke fingers in her growth
she hides beneath ripping cardigans
and discusses rain that locates her skin-
her mother teaches her to build
fences in her mouth- her sighs
are barbs atop kneeling strangers in transit
where her heart pastures

she holds her foot mid-step when they call her name
yowanina; mother taught her to be a lady
her mouth is a shelf for things dying
she grows out her dread-
locks to hold between her teeth
she was told a lady must never speak back
she laces her body into tongues
her walk is a sound of church drums

ii.

her father wishes away the moon
in his obsession with breaking things
he throws empty bottles into the night
for their crack, crack, cracking then
tiptoes to her bedside, his hushed tones
cutting through the dark like bread knives
he talks about god and his friends who've died
sniffs escape his throat like orphans in a lone city
she doesn't want her mother to wake
her chest is a cemetery she buries her father's head in
but graveyards are our way of never letting go
he rises like ghosts of things that still ring true
in her grieving ears; they mind-fuck her into believing
nothing is ever really dead
when father draws breath from her mouth,
worships the empty graves in her body
with his wood   (en) god

she turns her face to her younger sister,
a penitent choking down creeds,
she peers through the dark teeming across her bed
she can hear her youth breaking on knuckles of moans
her faith gritting its teeth
through blood as a kind of sainthood

iii.
she mascaras her eyes not to blink,
her stare is a fortification
of secrets
asking the clouds not to spit

she swallows the silver spoons in her mouth
that force-fed her ghosts
'til she was obese to her throat,
her ears drum, drum drumming stoic desolation
into hymns, her body is an empty church
calling a wanting man to his knees

screamed-out nights build walls
up her vagina, her legs creak
like revolving doors
opening into sore epiphanies

grief is like coming in from the noon sun

and everything is black and static

it is, but, for a moment

the preacher you sent to me

i.

the preacher you sent to me, lord, wore a yellow hat that bled
indifference into his eyes when he told me i had to be saved,
he tipped me off his tongue with a tilt of his head, lord,
where does a poor man buy a halo?

ii.

he comes by
sunday morning at temple street
and you know
from the church drums
rattling scales off your sleep deprived eyes,
the last sting of cold picking its blanket from the air
and shelving it at your feet
with the rest, you must offer your hallelujah

the neighbor shines his pair of Bata
you wonder how it feels
breaking into new shoes

iii.

the preacher you sent to me spoke in a singular white color,
told me that was the color of religion when it caught the fire
in my eyes, it burnt to black. he referenced death to my skin, i
always thought death in blood baking to blue, lord, his eyes
were winter rivers with hands in their pockets when he saw

my blanking face and called my hunger righteous while
holding out a collection plate.

he gave me a beaded collar to count at
on those sleepless nights
i lip-sing hail marys and hallelujahs
til my head hurts from choking back what i ought to pray

lord, all i wanted was a morsel to quiet the song in my
stomach. he gave me one portion of communion like jesus
would run out on a second serving.

iv.
you look at his face;
wrinkles concealed beneath vaseline
you wonder how many of your wounds would heal
beneath that layering
he compares your bleeding to jesus
and you wish your bones too weren't breaking

your hands pause their clapping
where everything he wears seems extravagant
you dwarf in his shadow
his smile full of teeth when again
he calls your poverty blessed
you wish a might in your failing hand
to reach out and break prayers upon them
tooth.by.tooth

his robes spill over the red earth
you touch your shoulders that are starting to shiver
you wonder if sunday would still be unkind
in a white robe spilling over itself
to blanket over your cold cold bones

mirages

he follows the sea in the highway
that keeps going   with the sun goes down
'til he's too far down to turn back
too far gone to remember home
he wanted to be a fisher of men

he follows the moon in the belly of the sea
that keeps digging   with the stroke of a wave
'til he's too deep to behold a breath
his mouth too full to say a prayer
he wanted to be a seafarer

he follows the tweet of a bird into the forest
the face of jesus into the halo
a petal, the foot of a wind, the grain of sand
'til he's too disturbed to think himself a poet

he smokes a cigarette,
urinates by a roadside shrub
he just wants to be a man

a house with a torn roof

mud walls and a reed mat

is still a house

woman of clay

you can tell in the way she moves her feet over a stone-
bed without making a sound, hushing a rattling
of pebbles with a stroke of toes,
the way she mourns with the mo(u)rning leaves
the way she bows to waves that she, was born
of a river that runs through a village churchyard.

she wields weeds upon the smooth of her tongue,
a fullness of sea brushes against her bosom
leaving no trace, she holds just enough
water to still her thirst to the next rain

she's grey and sticks through cracks and all gaping things
they look at her; her feet and the stretch of her stride
the lisp on her tongue that eats her words before they are said
her breasts, her bare back, her eyes

'there's no way to justify this waste'
they speak in sigh

they partition her body like she's a third world
state begging to be colonized
they assume she needs to be saved
by someone, a man, a god, a tube of lipstick

her maker flows on   to shores

where the water is full
with laughing children
and tired fathers

the village is yesterday
and the church is closed

she's a barren woman nursing a stone; she
wears barbed wire in her mouth
chains around her neck, her fingers, her belly
she's an artist's canvas begging hands to finger-
paint her
and pencils. and pencils. and pencils
'til she's out of razor blades

she's a pot spilling a neck of water
a brick house coming together at the beams

the flower pot calls her too raw to hold water
the house calls her weak
the potter molds   and breaks her
she yields   molds and breaks
she yields   and breaks
and breaks   and breaks

she takes a cutting, a drying, a heating
'til she's baked enough to be called worthy
'til she's hard enough to cut

i wave a henna-d hand to a passing kite

the child asks me
'if i combed my fingers through the clouds
what would i come up with?'

'a handful of rain i guess' i say

'is heaven made of rain?'
she angles her head in childlike wonder

'maybe. to a certain extent.'

'so how long will the rain be?'

'as long as heaven exists i suppose'
i sweep a hand over her brow to cut a breaking sweat

'your hand looks like a rainbow so close!'
she grins a spill of gold

heaven is one full rain above us

hush

a poor man's child cries like the open sea
she ripples arms of vishnu;
her prayer, a wave that simmers
off dry hands afraid
to die   a passive death

she's a blank journalist
leaving no black ink
on the hands of yet another december
and god is still transcribing her silence
where the wind still resents her hollow lungs
that clang like church bells
now hear her   roar

on her back, piscators sway
she calls *'whatevers'* to float their boats
their buoyancy rooted in her ability not to break
beating here, netting there,
rocking 'til she's all hooks and whips

they watch her; silver and grey
where a noon sun fences upon her skin
in hesitancy to dive to her undergrowth
she regurgitates blinding wishes like confessionals

a poor man's child is an open sea
on a day full of rain

like she wasn't already full enough
her roof is an open palm,
she remembers storms
in a full bloom garden of weeds

scavengers pick at her head
but never make nests and
tweet-tweet, they mock her disease
death buries itself in corral
depths she can still behold
'til her eyes are vacant
drive-through cemeteries
where ghosted humanitarians crowd
on her headstone
and bury her in mulch

a poor man's child is the rock at her feet
that refuses to die when they feed her
her own tears and call it holy water

the silence of a poor man's child is the cry
of a child giving birth to her own salvation

as the moon dismounts a saddle of trees

ruffling dewed leaves

the air cracks and chirrs like a distraught mistress

dawn buzzes like a hive on fire

all things minor

we are hand written
self-help stick notes
taking up space
in a journalist's handbook
beside fancy words
like inspirational
and poignant
and moving
they move us to raw graves;
our epitaphs only a meter to ratings

our backyards are bloated with field guns
claiming to protect
when all the leaves fall way too soon
and you stand there calling us helpless
when your gardens are ripe
-away-
far away from
-my home-   is not a home
on your tongue
it's the place where death goes to live we
have become indifferent to dying
praying for actual passing
than climbing virtual hills
into statistics of worthlessness
and poetry is kamikaze guns to our heads
that call us invisible

invisible
like many a young girl trapped
inside tar skins
you break them out
like premature zits
to cure your irritation
you curse their ugliness as
they melt inside your accents
thinking it means they're hot
they strip their dress
and their skin-
looking for self-worth
in your systematized untruths
impermanence tastes like one too many elegies

we are derivative conflicts
raking acrylic nails
through chalkboards
that write us sick
yes, we are sick-
of history that rides upon our legs
like mud stains
we curse perpetuity
like eve's sin begging
take us back
take us back to innocence
we straddle the border
of acceptance and optimism
waiting in a bed of sawdust
for a carpenter's son
to finish us

the night couldn't sleep.
i stood by the window
unconsciously stroking my pen
just so it didn't weep

the air was filled with cricket song
street lamps and neem

beyond a cloudless sky
stars purred
like a symphony orchestra

i felt myself belong to
a tangible heaven

where the night sings

let my feet not tremble

(there is a rain) that tumbles out of greyed eyes
digging holes through my pillow
stirring the scent of irredeemable pasts

(a stain) that tangles through my hair
the adhesive of lost years
a crust i can't cut off

(i weep) sifting dusted thoughts
on timbered breaths
perusing marlboro clouds

(i sleep) seeking rest
larger than the bouts of mania
clogging the gap between my knees

(i bow) spitting dejection
into the sun-baked grace
of incensed penitence

i hold scissors to the fabric of my irregular existence
cutting and reshaping impertinent squares
to fit an earth spinning on the balls of my feet

(i tremble) hands chalking narcotics
force feeding lead into paper thoughts
(i tremble) folding wordless prayers into barrels

i, am an unfinished war; restless and muddied-
an unsung hallelujah on the mouths of runaways

o that unspoken words were armour
where darkness wields swords to a heart
beating through the walls of a dead-end street
where nights die lesser deaths

(please) write me into the gospel of gentiles
that jesus swung by my rear view mirror
but never touched my face

and when i go, *(please)* let my feet not tremble

tonight the moon didn't show

the sky was blank. the poem read- a black moon

**but what's another bullet-
point**

underneath the color?

braces can't contain this grinding of teeth

at twelve, she's an iron sequence
umpiring a game of thumbs and teeth
that leaves her awfully tempted
to pull them out and peck at gravel
before she's judged for their crookedness

at fifteen, the demons growing inside her rib cage
are starting to manifest into strongholds above her chest
the boys start to notice her in their addiction to irregularity

'keep going!' they preach
she grows out her toes to fit the shoes
laid out for her, her feet move forward
to anywhere but her self
she's tilting her head at eighteen
to fit the smoke rings over her head   into halos

at twenty five, she's waking up to die of the silence
rusting through her body like bone cancer
do you hear that -the sound of god dying
at twenty six, she murders herself inside her spoken word
and feeds her pieces to soulless scavengers

this is her waking up at 3pm
and this is the darkness that seals her death
she's a full-sized woman inhaling an empty bag
of samson left by an almost stranger
inside her glove compartment

sundays are claustrophobic; she's a woman run out of salt

her sweat tastes like waterfalls, its static steadying into song
upon the roof of -her mouth- is broken at the seams
cursing at birds prophesying 'beautiful',
beautiful are the feet tiptoeing past her door
to preach peace elsewhere

night skies shroud her with darkness
when beneath their skirts flashes a white holiness
she's a freckled mustang trying to outrun
the large-mouthed daydream eating through her rear view
mirror

my father had taught me how to wield a spear

when i returned home, mother eyed down my scars, sighed

look how beautifully you've unlearned

the deaths of your fathers

blackout night poetry (mixed vignettes)

i.
as the rain runs restless hooves
across the roof
fading into thin walls,
pain slips through
the torn pockets of my eyes
    i feel it belong
    inside my skin

ii.
silence sits in a large bottomed mug luke-
warm and bitter;
wending its way
through clenched teeth
    careful not
    to knock her knees

iii.
a candle burns by the bed stand
yellow flame flickering
blue halo crowning a blushed red wick

i want to write a poem
full of such light
and such colour

but as my pen touches the pad,
shadows kiss the ballpoint

'til

blackened words
cover the page
like an eclipse

iv.
the stench of despair
seeps through the keyhole
the gap beneath the door
the space between the panes of my window

like blood through a bandage
exuding from the wound
beneath my synthetic layering of skin

v.
my thoughts are a choir of crows
tapping limp feet on bloodied floors

i ask them to teach me
the language of night skies

but all they bring
is dry grass
and some dirt

vi.
tiny birds eat into a quiet dawn
with loud mouthfuls
tweeting and slurping
on an orange sun
saddled to aluminum rooftops

magetha ma mwere (season of harvest)

nigh is the harvest season, magetha ma mwere
yellowish-brown leaves envelope the ranges of mt. kenya
aspen-fiery heads of sagging grain beckon
maidens to wield their pick knives

beaming like escaped suns, they descend the hills
usurping a nightingale's ballad, they cut like well-greased
machines
reaping into a reddened night sky, where they return home
arrayed in the pride of filled baskets balancing on their heads

the vales of Igara

through remnants of a harvest moon
a rooster boasts his cries
the village arises to wonted tune
in the vale, the sun lies
in wait for the maidens of Igara
pots upon their brow, downhill, they swagger

her beaded legs strew a folk-song
o'er the goat-path; wild flowers dance
wring their fingers in puddled throng
in dawn's lure, she sways in trance
inside the flames of the msasa trees
the river calls in gentled wheeze

she dips her pot in the pristine waters
her head haloed in a garland of colour
wine-red, amber, green leaves, they saunter
a topsy-turvy wind, they collar
she lays a tune onto the river
in ephemeral waves, refrains waver

in ephemeral waves; a rusty leaf
an abandoned page, a mud fish
skulk into the reef
a muttered wish
sinks on a silver coin
of a lad's heart she longs to purloin

rays cut through the canopy
casting a silhouette upon the water.
in the msasa branches, against gravity
the lad perches, arrows in quiver
with intention so stark
she straightens her back

she should stay, listen to his ode
but at home awaits the day's load

the night is holy no more

we've been singing awfully loud

    the lion is harvesting our garden- again

we became song, monotonous with drums in our stomachs

there's only so many ways you can arch your lip pretending
to while away distress, making sense of static on a rusty
panasonic

but this   -blank   is a look i give a person
telling me to pray and all will be well
the drums bellowing, weaving knots and rumbling
through hollow stomach walls-
that's no sound of manna crashing onto desert rocks

the village wrote us into song
            poverty is a sin, poverty is a dog,
            it has no grace, poverty is you

there's only so many fingers you can stick in your ears
pretending not to listen. hands on cheek, sleet eyes-
but this   -glare-   is the look i give someone
saying poverty is not lack of food but a state of mind
souls flee through crumbling bones, jumping from rib to
skull
stomachs eat into backs, curving us into question marks at
thirteen

how do you expect a hungry child to believe in god

when their hands are holding down their stomachs

instead of being lifted up to heaven?

**i will not just sit here harvesting rain with my tongue...
anymore (i)**

the first twenty five years of my life
grandma told one recurrent story,
albeit it shrunk with subsequent editions
scorched words in ailing whisper

i. june 1993 (a giggly three-year old toddler perched on her
knee, sparks launch like fireworks from an outside fire
throwing us into a fit of laughter that rings, reverberates and
fades through the ranges of Igara)

i was a horse in my bloom, wild like the glint in your eye
                         she recounts
during the war, you, slung over my shoulder
your mother bursting with child
we folded our skirts, ran miles
singing war songs across the Nile
refrains bouncing off the riverbed
            o fire is burning, fire will burn
            fire will reach the enemy and he shall confess
            fire will cleanse and warm
            o fire is burning, fire will burn

tupambane zaidi (let's intensify the struggle)
            we'll shed blood until there is enough to cleanse the
soil-
            we shouted over raised machetes and spear vi-
            cious rage seeking peace

the sieved satisfaction when we returned home five years later

wounds the size of war, we salted with glee
your father never came out of that bush
but what honour to die for your country!

(in premeditated dreams, i was the hero with a life on the line)

ii. january 1999 (under the jack-fruit tree at the village square,
the village congregates. hanging onto every word from a man
in camouflage. a hope tagging at every lip)

how long shall we wait to receive our portion?
the fire we built burned but our hands are stiff with cold

camouflage man speaks;
      we fought for you, brought peace
      no more bloodshed, spears are ornaments in your homes
      and we continue to fight
      for your health, your education, your life
      where is the gratitude?

grandma shakes her head
`what's a hospital with no medicine
a school with no learning
little butts warming benches'
big whoop, you stacked up bricks, nailed roofs atop'

iii. january 2005
camouflage man speaks
      what peace we brought
      young men and women
      criminals roaming the streets hand in pocket
      will we stand and watch them burn our reign down
on rolled up cigarettes

iv. november 2009 (having tea, legs stretched, hand pinned onto the living room mat. damp eyes, teargas reeking from the street)

"close the door, trees have ears," grandma whispers

v. december 2015 (slouched on a floor mattress in a hospital corridor –three days- waiting for a medic)

"my child, listen and listen good.
be your father's daughter.
they'll come at you with guns
but there's something mightier"

the words like blades, cut their way up her throat *-cough, cough, wheeze-* consuming her into their mist

vi. i shall not sit here warming bar stools, blotting ink on serviettes
come with me,
let us spill ink until the image is clear and loud enough
if blood is to spill, well, let it spill 'til we are drained -all out-
what's life anyway if not to be given for another

and i've seen the northern sky
and the masai mara sunset

but nothing ever beautiful as the smile

of a just eaten child

a bohemian boy with a shimmy in his step

you're the reason
for the itch in my brain
to mimic the click in your laugh
that clatters, halts for a lungful
then pops, bustling through vales on ascent

a mango develops in my throat
envy and ache for the reflex flicker
as you gaze beyond cosmic canopies

lately it's hard to fall asleep
sadness clogs the air
the darkness inside my sockets has
never been so daunting

maybe
it's your earth-marinated legs
that glide then shimmy
plodding washed down gravel
knocking- nudging- i realize that wasn't a dance
seeing the dents in our existences

or
it's the bop in your tum
that rumbles like percussion
malnutrition playing butterfly
ribs threatening to pop out
each time you flash that nervous grin

possibly

the strings of hope nesting in your threadbare pants
the clouds stuck in your teeth
the litanies muffled in your melodies

azure lakes, satiated skies veiling the country-scape
will never be the same
sly winds whisper a different creed

mine is a pen gone native
to feed a child 'til he breaks into dance
as he teaches me to laugh -bohemian style-

the plight of a refugee

sunday mornings, dad would sit by the porch, steady eyes peering above half-moon reading glasses propped against his nose, shouting through the spring breeze for us not to go too far. we'd mimic his head-shake in a cackle of laughter that bobbed from hillside to hillside as we chased after butterflies fluttering through shrubs until we were dehydrated enough to hear mum calling us for lemonade. this is not one of those days. dad walks two days ahead of us hoping to intercept death and mum has nothing to offer to our failing stomachs and her bones, her bones clank like empty pans being stacked away onto a shelf. we wish to cry to god but who can lift their swelling tongue to pray?

**i will not just sit here harvesting rain with my tongue…
anymore (ii)**

this house is no shelter; no doors, no vents,
just holes in the thatch sneaking in gasps
of recycled air we forgot how to breathe

mothers crying out, giving up life as they give life
children taught what to say and what not to think
young men in a deficit of hope watching roofs cave in

and you say "we held guns, fought for peace"
o why thank you! but we've run out of gratitude
scraped knees out of blood and prayer

there are no pots boiling on many a stove
kids sift through city bins; indistinct shadows
in a fog tapping rain with their tongues

i shall not stow my pen; throw my hands in the air like I don't
care

bring sticks, bring oil
bring matches and those paper poems,
let us start a fire, burn this house down
til' it's warm enough to be called a home

an empty plate, a drought

a prayer- fast d(r)ying

on the lips of a child

beauty and nothingness

sometimes i get lost inside my writing hand
for it to wrap me in its fist and punch me into a wall

the pen leaves me hollow as a pin-pricked egg
its water piles at my feet
until i'm convinced i am made of rain
god could have made me a cloud
but my imperfect curves refuse to wear silver

the poets congregate speaking of petals
conceding splendour to littered sidewalks
they write city trucks into saviours
plunking hymns in their choked-up wail

and what am i?

a shimmy shaken off a leaf into an unlistening air
if the wind could shut up, you'd hear the sound of my pen
but she combs her fingers through my   (h)air and
comes out full of herself

so i write of dried lilies. and of beauty rooted in nothingness

my grocery lists are bloated with words that don't grow here
like pistachios and manna
and even if they did, i could never afford them
so i write them into letters to god
i never have the courage to mail *(dear lord!)*

my poetry is a left-handed attempt at self-healing

i still suck at playing doctor- the white sheets always too short
to cover all of my blackness *(dear lord!)*

i'm a blister on the hand of an ordinary day
a glass moon, monkey-gripping on the west side of heaven
you'll have to cut my fingers to stop me from reaching out

westward bound

the kettle was starting to hiss at the stove
i stood by the window gazing at a journeying sun

twilight sauntered on jelly legs
raising a trail of dust with her sepia gowns

stars were beginning to trickle into the celestial square
in peachy-yellowed twos and threes

in the valley, chimneys blew out puffs of smoke
to a flock of home bound crows

the wind gathered her children
and sang them to sleep on measured undertone

everything was headed west
where things go to die
at least for a while

i made wishes on passing planes and cracking knuckles
for the chill of dusk to draw blood from my fleshed pain

by the couch, despair sat unshaken,
round and voluptuous,
flipping through a dog-eared book

the kettle was starting to boil by the stove
coffee claimed the air, bitter and sharp

i took a swig, burning and acrid,
but that
was still much easier to swallow

an elegy of sorts

i.

yet another moonless night, i sit with the lights on afraid the
dark seeping from beneath my wooden bed will suffocate me
dare i close my eyes in sleep. for when i go, i envision blank
faces staring down my limp body in the rough-and-ready tee and
frayed short pyjamas. notice the reddening face of one
that tore a ligament jumping over the hill of unwashed
clothes erupting on my bedroom floor. the flaring nostrils
that discovered the pile of unwashed dishes moulding in the
sink. but woe is one who finds the self-hate stacked in neat
piles on the bookshelf. the days i spent documenting green
envy, working and reworking those toxic metaphors, tearing
out the rough edges until hate was a pretty fur coat hanging
on the rack ready to go out. and boy was the outside chilly

ii.

will the ache in my poetry remind anyone of the psalms
that sin is not always yellow with disease
and black can be beautiful in metaphors that wither
like wild flowers on the brow of an outcast

iii.

the priest rushes worn safari boots through ecclesiastes 12
to pass the collection plate round   and everything that has
breath
is still in motion that i never quite comprehend
even my verses, i'm told, are breathless

iv.

through the stained window
i search a star littered air
for my next lungful

v.
the poet calls me beautiful

vi.
my depression is blue as a cloudless day
she thunders metered syllables through my breakdown
like a tow truck dragging pieces of me on the tip of her
tongue
the audience strums tiny violins between thumb and third
finger
at her prowess to make my agony look like art

vii.
i hold ink-stained fingers
to the neck of death
feeling for a pulse

seasonal footnotes

i.
migrating birds pitch camp on my roof
i punch pen-holes into the screen transcribing their tongues
so many colours, and notes to steal-
alien feathers, to stick in a h(e)a(r)t

ii.
i'm landlocked on a minor pathway
giving misspelt directions to singed hikers
in khaki shorts and ripped t-shirts
i'll barter the dust creeping up their legs
for one blue-skied poem

iii.
the singing follows the poets to sea
leaving me a ringing of walls
and lukewarm feet that lie and linger:
i'm a slave to self-deception
justifying myself inside pharmaceutical recipes

iv.
my poetry blushes with yellow indifference
it falls out of my mouth like baby teeth
rusting through a severe case of icing
and jiggles to the woo song of rats

v.
i'm a footnote weaving itself into a cocoon
as poetry mocks my weakness to satisfy her greed.
pitchy metaphors like downtown whores
beg me to penetrate them deeper- faster- harder!

vi.

nest-less birds night binge on crickets depopulating the grass
until the silence is loud enough to hear itself. i'll bite my nails
and even that will sound poetic in the tips and taps popping
off into the still night, if you asked me to write, i'd only ask
for a blank page

i asked a cannon mouth to speak to me of love

grandma once asked me to start a fire

my hand held keys in a gathering of wood and a
strike of matches

satisfaction swelled up my face as the house hummed
and yellows spilled over shadows of wrinkles
digging through her cheeks

'a rumble does not a fire make', she said
a fire that is true speaks a whisper, silent as a clowder's march

it is the sound that love makes-
like red ants, she rallies her flame
to the feet of a forest- a stamp
of silence over a crickets' refrain

'blot out the smoke', grandma said
what have rain clouds brought you
except shield your face from god

you look like a storm when you blink it away

a boy once told me   -i-   like a storm, was beautiful
his voice, a song of bird that littered the grey of my eyes with
spark
his words crept upon me like a sneeze skirting lonesome
breaths over my skin
excuse me- i blessed his plea

he wielded a wrist of tenors
and i-   was a child at a gathering of kites
tugging invisible strings to a song that gets to say hold on

he bellowed a prayer that makes a woman fall in love
and we-   loved like rain

i began falling when he stopped calling

me sunshine; lost my grip on heaven
but the earth was too hollow to contain me
i balled against its walls like a whistle mid-blow

grandma told me
'love, like fire when true, speaks a whisper'

revolving doors

some days i wake up all fluid.
like a speck of dust dancing in mysterious currents
resting on a reaching leaf, an indiscernible existence -green on
the edge
or on a winding road -- one with the pack -losing self

other days, i land on an open eye – friction
spreading distress like grit
i'm thrown out in disdainful waterworks.

those days, i worship rain
the kind that digs ditches
shrinks bones, delves into vast blanks
it shrieks and shrills
like hammers crashing into rocks
-to mud. to me.

it rouses a staleness of death/rotting leaves
i'm sinking into this solid mess
inundated in rain's waking
grey threads winding from liquid skies una-
dulterated insanity
the last time i ran out of salt

i'll never tell if i'm going or coming
if i'm the blossom peering from the cracks
or just the runoff

odyssey

i scurry hither and thither
to escape the larging thunder

but you're in the wind
and your name hangs
before my comma-arched mouth
        -waiting-
it lingers in the air
fluttering in unbelief
of a potholed day

i metamorphose
from the chrysalis of self-conscious
turpitude that holds me
inside its walls

i'm believed
a child of trouble
despair shoves her
breast between my teeth to stop
me from crying

when sorrow labours long enough
it births child
with knees too beat they refuse to stand

at the heart of a scab
there i'm found
        seeking
salvation in leftover blood

journal of feet that wonder (i)

prayer feels like paperclips
steel and frigid
yellows and blues
strung together in a pretty band
that refuses to hold my hair still

perhaps i'm weathered
into bone ash
seeing as i lift
weightless as feathers
sojourning in pharaoh's desert

sure, a watered land is beautiful
look at all the greys
in their stirring
 and the greens
in their stilling

i'm birthed in the spine of a whirlwind
in the womb of dead things
leaves and browns
grit and twigs
i emerge in their cracking
where holy water spills
from my wine-skin

journal of feet that wonder (ii)

i scuttle across the plain of sharon
open palms and grazed knees
flirting with crocus yellows and violets

predawn chants a meek song
as the desert scales itself of petals

the wastelands are speckled with puddles
mud red-
they call to me

i'm a toothless infant
toddling toward the heart of god

journal of feet that wonder (iii)

we are spoken
off the same heathen tongue
crying-
we are dying

our souls
are white-threaded
-storms
coming down

we are standalone invisibles
clinging onto walls

and hard wood floors
and dusty streets

because
in a way

in their rigidity
and their dimness
and their speechlessness

they remind us
of us

cursive

i.

at the edge of a charcoal painted night is a puppet-mouth
moon choking feathers down its throat to the kind of static
that stutters and stills -of waiting, waiting for an abyss to
finish needling its skirts and cover me in the grunting- the
groaning of stones landing upon my face, i'm still breathing in
the winking of pebbles- an invisible bug excavating home
beneath debris of fallen glory- crying- where is mercy in these
echoes bang-banging through my hollow hands and finding
cooing not song

ii.

my right(ing) hand hurts from bleeding words into each
other, my poetry reads retarded stealing breath from readers
that never meant to stay- stay- why would they- in words that
tremble leaving a lesser mouth- afraid to stop lest the dryness
glues it shut altogether- i speak in cursive calling jesus, jesus-
afraid to stop lest i hear him beckoning me in the silence- i
only speak the language of noise- words fire through my
hands like heated air if you look close enough my poetry claps l
ike thunder

iii.
ralph, it crawls up sore-
throat leaving a bitter taste
upon my larynx

iv.
you're pretty fine, they say to me in places i'm seen, usually
alone or not at all, i am invisibility's manifest failing to
become art, a labyrinth of doodles, of upstrokes and down
strokes, littering a canvas face and never sinking to the floor
you'll have to sew my mouth shut to stop me from speaking

v.
grace is told in the procession of liquid words escaping eyes
that blink pain down with a meekness of feathers- falling- as
if angel wings flapping upon an altar before which i stand
choking on a mouthful of scripture that stacks me into a
high-rise edifice with a closer view of heaven

vi.
rain starts its falling
where my feet tip their ending
like eagles in soar

mweine maawe (child of my mother)

for Catherine

i.
her courage is a wild weed
with her roots close
the july sun can't tame
the yellow of her budding

her grace is neem ascending
up a midnight air
with the perseverance
of a tea cup sitting to cool

ii.
she holds her own barbed wire
when she jumps through fences
only she can stretch
the measure of breadth of her back

iii.
she lifts ashen hands to her face
pretending to warm her fingers
in the fire of her eyes

it's cold in november
and her flame is turning blue

every blow is an exhaled prayer

iv.
her prayer is a bird song
hijab-ed among leaves of trees

she
is a bird caged
too long, it stops chirping
to contemplate the latch

her cage-r
is an open mouth of flies
as cows come home

ado [looking back]

you'll probably never learn how to start a poem
and your work will be good at best
but that should be good-
enough to sit you up at night

don't point your pen towards your wrist
your words are heavy, doused in blood
charcoal- coal maybe, you look coherent in black ink

the backyard of your childhood home is a swing-less
plantation
but you'll carry the buzz of bees off banana flowers,
the violet of sun-dried sap in your hair
and a handmade fibre doll
that will have no room on your city night stand

but look

look at the colours until they speak.
search, search between the blacks and whites,
and there, there you'll find the voice of god, -still-
don't look back, ado, we're not out of salt, yet

so don't, don't be in a hurry to get there
because you won't wanna stay
and home will be the swing in your arms
that never stilled

i dig you graves inside my poems ~ you've become immortal

nights creak along to worn-out mornings
cowled in foggy blankets
too tepid to be clever
too brittle to be coveted

coffee tastes like you
nippy and metallic
like the gingerly click of the door
when you left
without a word
shoving a gag into my mouth

i search through liquids for answers
where my heart drowned
in your sea eyes

i sit in bed
digging graves
inside wretched poems

thinking

there's got to be a better way to bury you
without biting welts into my cheeks
to muzzle the waterworks

how do i write your epitaph
without invoking you

memories of you fall like leaves
onto my dwindling path
settling
rotting
into mulch

growing a life of their own

you are a jumble of roots
and shoots
some mornings i see you
through broken windows
pink and yellow blossoms at your core

the neighbors call you flowers

beneath the veil of dusk
you wilt into pages
words excavating like shovels
sweat raining onto metaphors
till my room reeks of death

i dig you graves
but you've become immortal

walls

tonight i'll build
all those
uncried tears
into walls
and like all strongholds
lie in shadows
in wait
for wrecking
balls and earthquakes
and other god hands
to tear me down
all over again

samsara [passing through]

coming out in birth
from a tepid waterbed in the shadows
my paper crown evanesced
as i hula-hooped through a ring-of-fire
falling headfirst into an intricacy
of lighthouses in mouths of strangers
inclined over my cot throne
blinding me before i could see the
sweaty faced woman
that housed me rent-free
in her chambers for nine months
spelling out love's first lesson

that night i stuck a thumb in a ditch
between my cheekbones
the woman with a sun on her brow
didn't allow me to fathom hunger
she shoved ridges beneath my tongue
that's the first time i saw the face of god
i remember
nights became blurred
whenever she left my field of vision

(she's the reason i still sleep with lights on)

a village would then raise me;
that loud-mouthed gong preaching a gospel of *don'ts*
and *'no she didn't'*

scorn slipped through clenched jaws
shooting rusty arrows into my mouth,
the first time i tasted death
it smelled like red dust in a drizzle
the grit scrubbing my throat in condemnation-
i smoked cigarettes to mask the stench
coughing up a wheeze with each drag
but boy was i glad to drown the thunder playing my eardrums

i digress
i should be redeeming myself here
i'm counting times i've died
funny how it's as many times as i've resurrected
but i never document that
except on rainy days
that remind me of the sun trapped on the brow of my mother
that reminds me of rain
that reminds me of the sun trapped on the brow of my
mother

i digress
you know how rain falls the day you forget your umbrella
and tangles your hair into a web of kinks
you hear your thoughts washed down in the runoff
to a stagnant pool inside your chest where they decay

i swallow pain and courage like seeds
hold them in the nursery beneath my ribs

and let them grow
till they are tall enough to kiss the sun on the brow of my
mother
till they are strong enough to define me

inside the breath that creates me

the moon jumps from branch
to branch in the blacking tree
that glooms the night
i can't find my feet
in the shadows that buoy me
and i'm done searching a day
that baptizes me invisible

i will be beautiful in december
when the yellow of pain
buds upon an ashen earth
and isn't guilty for its rolled fist
that refuses to wave to a flirting wind

let this fire not pass me by
i wish between thumbs
and when i can't
wish it   i ask it and
when i can't ask it,
i pray it
        -this fire-
that hearths my breath
until i can't pray it
but there are no diamonds
to be found in the breathlessness
of an aborted prayer

a charcoal-painted façade

beneath our indefinite day
feet swallow the plump of shadows
as bones creak in their drying
she won't move-
afraid to start a fire

she's the poster child
for bad poets
rhyming a ceiling
to a rain's falling
she wields an earth
inside her wri(gh)ting hand
and casts it in black helvetica
as the hand of simplicity
chokes at her throat
--you are a liar
-you are a liar
it buries it's nails
into her chest
she's a coffin at the fifth
pondering a resurrection
for a woman tired of bleeding

tired-

as a day that lands
feathered feet
upon her hand

finding her too beat to
make a wish
angels hang their heads
with the shadows on the wall
they found her too lazy
to fall in love

it's october
and she wonders
if the church is still open.
she watches the growing trees
and wonders
if they ever sawed a
large enough pew
to sit all of her baggage

it's october
she has gained
another ten pounds
and still has nothing
but empty hands
to put on the collection plate
it's october
and pews are still cold
the sun still preferring
the roof of a church
to the cold hearts of outcasts

six pm reduces her to bone ash

she's still too heavy
for a pack-rat breeze
some nights
she ponders the lightness of clouds
and how something so weightless
can hold so much water
she falls asleep to
their falling
stealing passive breaths from the
prayers of saints

days well

and shrink

like nomad clouds

between sky and ground,

she weaves gutters

of bones, feathers and dirt

where rain writes petrichor psalms

bethel

i crouch inside a teardrop

i.
dawn skies are flamethrowers
leaving no cure in the blitz
of debris carpeting
the plain face of a passing day
caking on the taut of my knuckles

ii.
poison words creep at me
like a garden of weeds
eating out of my right hand
my body buds opium violet
seeking poetic correctness
in morphine verse

iii.
my identity has become leafy
from the tepidness of pretending
 i'm fine. i'm fine i'm fine
if you look too closely
the blossom is but regular weeds
dyed another shade of disease
and the chirping of birds
is the sound of teeth crunching
through dried out untruths

iv.
i spectate the demise of laughter
in a phlegm of apologies

coughed out into rolled fists of bless
you! *sante!*
their edge-less prayers don't cut it

v.
the lamp's buried in the guilt
of unspoken prayers

i rest my load on a ballpoint
seeking redemption in
hourglass whisper-
a back-and-forth shuttling of sighs

listen

goat hour confessional

the glass windows veil themselves in layers of night
i crawl between their walled blackness-
that ravages my eyes to a redness

      -i sigh-
how wrong they were about me,
i am not dead- yet, of the bloodshot

that manifests like sin, scarlet,
in loose duffel bags i get to carry nowhere
    maybe they were right
i plague my bed like fleas
biting into nothingness
on those nights when god
 is lost between the sheets
whispering   'look how i love you'
all i see is the nihilism
of a bed that hasn't been made in weeks
and denting in places
not deep enough
to contain all the heaviness
    i tell mother i'm okay
when really all i want to say
is i'm sick and tired of being inadequate
she still loves me
like my mother loves me
telling me god is enough
    -i pray-
the only way i know how to love her
all the while thinking
no way god is listening to the gibber

of a vain being
        i've mastered indifference
of speaking to walls and calling jesus
just in case he's somewhere
lost in the rejection notices
plastered over my face.
to be honest
        i'd rather lift hands
than these un-picturable words
like manic depression and anxiety
i can't put up in my room
since i took out all the nails
not to hang jesus back up
on an air-signed cross
i toss off my index finger
 into a teeming darkness
dear lord,   *is there a way*
            to be honest
and still be considered poetic
i spit into a puddle of sunshine
on my bedroom floor
and watch the yellow of disease
rise like the Nile in april
        -float away-
i hear the song of water weed
building webs in my hair
        'here'
bottom feeders call to me
i decide i'm tired of dysthymia
sitting at the verge of insanity
like the pew in the back of a church
calling 'jesus'

in words often fleeting
between euphoria and vestigial traces of shame
confessions and collection plates
through this and more,
can you hear me?

the sky was beginning to brown
soaking in an auburn sun

rundown engines sauntered by
like worker ants

at the potholed sidewalk
i bent, lacing my shoes

wheezing and waiting

dusk pulsed like a dying wave

i found them grey

i kicked the hungry child
into the webs weaving beneath my bed
his feet jigger in the dust rusting
off my bedpost where he stalls- tethered

i keep tricks in bags beneath my eyes
while my heart wilts in an open hand basket
i'm a ventriloquist tagging at the strings
of a tear drop while a mute button advances
down sore throat pleading repent, repent,
repent! the noise of its silence renders me deaf
in both ears i'm spent-

friday morning, sitting in my bed wishing
i was somewhere, somebody
in the least someone else

life walks by-
a dawdling procession of paper planes
launched off the agitated hand of a museless writer
they unfold mid-air, blank and creased
like the faithless renegade i'm become
feigning grace, sometimes humility
to sneak me past the afterglow
of a once fine day colour-fading through recollection

five days tonight, i left jesus on the kneeler
my self, in a streaking of headlights
and inexpensive noises
swishing and popping
past bubble-gum swallowing years
till i'm lost in the collapse of noon shadows-
scaling beneath butterfly wings
into storm clouds solemnly swearing
i found them this grey

la joconde

he turns the lights off
talks of prelim works of creation
of god
tipping buckets of black paint.

in darkness, he stumbles
to the wall where i'm superimposed
an inanimate object
gaze fixed on his intensity

a sort of mortal deity
brush in hand
twilight peering through the blinds
ricochets off his red hair

stroke to stroke
chocolate skin, brown eyes
a tame afro, native feet
stepping into his canvas

he models me to porcelain perfection

soon, his eyes are arrows
digging holes in my skin
finding nothing underneath

he seeks to fill in
the wince in my cheek
the crease crawling up the corner of my eye

i let him

his filbert
thrusting, scumbling, poking
but never hard enough to finish me
never hot enough to melt me

my hands are hooks
gathering a wrap at my belly
when they'd rather pin him to my bosom

skin on skin
his tongue a fetter
capsizing me in his waters

i want him to turn on the lights
lick litanies off my lips
catch a faith

o dieu! mon dieu!

he rolls tobacco in a rizla
chugs a whiskey
shudders a tempest

my eyes regurgitate rain

he arcs the corners of my mouth
glazes my cheek
then hangs me out to dry

a mystic existence

strangers rake their eyes over me
searching for clues
or punch lines
guessing through my emotions

she smiling or just coy
she beautiful or a temptress

i'm wondering where i went wrong

becoming masochist

my verse is a tragedy of foreign languages
crackling off a stuttering tongue
but this is by no means an apology

august is a reincarnation of january nightmares-
burnt-brick red skies plague the evenings
like wild flames of a premature hell
i insert a mantra like prayer into a thesaurus
dear. lord. sovereign
'til words of praise are too expensive
to launch off the lips of a poor man

(i digress)

today, i did week-old dishes
and cut myself on finger nails reaching for soap
my blood tanged like an alloy of steel and rust
to a desperate mouth stifling a stirring of pain

but my blood is still red
--beating
to the song churning in my empty belly

so if you ask me
i'm doing mighty fine

a high-rise somewhere north

(for Dave)

here is how i know

there's a sea beyond my eyes-

he writes of tall waters
that leave me craving for salty things
i'm convinced there is a sea
in there somewhere

      know this-
if ever i try to convince you
about the blueness of water
or steepness of cliffs
know that i'm a pirate
of the pure sky he builds
a little ways north-

his words are a spinning
of wool
and i wonder if it's still
raining in Dublin

his is the hand that rips petals
off cores and spreads it
as far as his breath will blow
and says *'here,*

see the magnitude of splendour
when you spread it all around'

and i know you've been told
that good things come in small spells
but he's taught me that a good heart
is one given in its fullness.

and he says to those wingless cores
'turn around- show them

how *plain* is all things royal-

and he says *'strip it all away- those*
anthers and the stigma-
strip it all away and see how

eternal we can be'

and like
if you are ever to pray,
 i pray you,
wear your knees to a bruise
just like if you're ever to write
 his words are a stacking
of high-rise stories
boasting scars in their triumph

and i'm convinced
beautiful are the feet
of him in haste to stop
and rummage for unpolished stones

among the dirt that he calls precious

and love-   is the tiptoe
around chaos that won't stop pacing-
his words are the quietus thunder
boasting the ring of truth upon his finger
'hush- do you hear the song inside that storm?'

i've seen a soul so mild
but what do you call one so meek
he inherits an earth to give it to another?
 i call him blessed because he has blessed

me with a thing to count

each night sleep is a far fetch

indent

by the doorknob
my hand aches in pause
afraid to wake the imprints
of a thousand sighs that
on occasion
blessed and cursed
into the cordial grey
of a mute host.
my body dug
a grave in the bed
i keep tabs
under the pillow
to stay afloat
they still won't
understand why
i skip
my meds
to exercise
a distressed heart
defending its relevance
in self-victimization
you tell me to count
blessings, i count syllables
in the breaking of hearts
i wear on a sleeve
where mine was ripped
each hand pulling a thread
as they walked away
to unravel some skin

i was told that's what
defines womanhood
and maybe i did
become
woman
when i took to bleeding
words too red
to be poetic
i sponged them down
with sawdust prayers
that only left me
bloated with questions
that dug me deeper
until the indent in the mattress
looked like me
imperfections and all
the mirror came
to bed with me
and suffered me
insomnia.
agoraphobia
pitched camp
on my nightstand
i got nowhere to go
if i can't sleep
so don't call me a coward
for staying in today
and yesterday
and the past four years
i was taught to follow
only where
there was a dream

he steals my footsteps and sculpts whistles

i tiptoe through a field of thistles
hands chained to my pockets' deep
by the river, crickets tongue their whistles

they recite a hymn as in the missal
tacked away in shadow's keep
i tiptoe through a field of thistles

the night is littered with epistles
love songs cling to my lip
by the river, crickets tongue their whistles

from the riverbank, a boy launches a missile
to my spinning disposition; feet caught in sweep
i tiptoe through a field of thistles

in the midnight breeze, his hair bristles
twinkling eyes drink me in gallant sip
by the river, crickets tongue their whistles

under the starry quilt, we nestle
treading love's threshold hip to hip
i tiptoe through a field of thistles
by the river, crickets tongue their whistles

the pipers have cased their song

i.

as the sun slumped deeper into the cushioned skyline, the
soles of my feet purpled with mileage. the scraggy children of
my optimistic youth sat by the porch steps singing a salted
hymn into the cracks that were starting to bleed. their 'sit
back, free your feet' chorused attempt at comfort seemed to
leather me black and blue in regret of the fluid time i once
spilled into dusted thoughts afraid of sore throat. i used to
blame my insomnia on the countability of sheep, now i can't
sleep over the hay of thoughts, wet and moulding inside. dear
children, if you're to pipe me a dirge, let it be grey and full of
woe. let the notes squeak and squeal, the noise of a life lived
out of tune

ii.

some days were almost normal

iii.

i made my bed and did the dishes. even started a book on a
dark skinned girl, striking, with a full set of pearl white teeth. i
named her *wish*, in a water baptism complete with a black
robed priest. she loved pickle sandwiches and bukowski
poems. i wrote her legs long and slender, her hair a kinky-fro.
she had a quick wit about her, someone you'd think nice,
even beautiful-

iv.

you know, everything i wasn't

v.

i killed her on a monday afternoon, let the black of her skin
close in on her under the july sun, her pleading cry raising
an octave, then caving into death like bad jazz

with blood caked on my brow
and an arch in my smile
i left the book- unfinished!

the children piped a victorious hymn as the ghost of my past
lay lifeless in my disappearing shadow

vi.

i have lapsed into nothingness
that thin line between dying and being
 i walk, like a tight rope

the children have cased their pipes
for there is no red border song
between green and black

feet that wander

no space left in the sky's pocket for the swelling of rain-
clouds
they came pooling at the pilgrim's feet 'til her bones shrieked
like the singing of swans

she thought

the plight of a nomad isn't the crossroad of synonyms
or the auto-correct weighing her spoken word on scales
while the wounds in her hand cake her staff in muddied
blood

tears streamed down her body into the dust
soaping her eyes in petrichor

the sun scorched puffy white clouds into grey
that loomed 'til blackness closed in on her iron rage
the moon lazed back into the fluff picking residues of light
to glorify her existence

the pilgrim resigned her hands to her squeaking back
praising the defiance of a firmament
that didn't bury her in the gravel beneath her feet
where she begged take me, take me, take me now
only halting to awe when through the rumbling thunder
she heard the restrained sniffles of a weeping jesus

stiff-necked years run through my fingers leaving no drops to wet the page

the hourglass since became anorexic, chiming grey sand prayers to shadows in the night. the walls i once claimed in portions of my verse have eaten into the one thing i believed myself to be, a silhouette dancing to a flicker of light from a passing car, they dig their teeth into my flesh, my heart sits cold in the rumble of their bellies afraid to dance. the years when a young sun washed over our red brick house, when i hugged a slow wind to the doorstep so we'd share an orange drink of sun, where did they go, i cry. the last note she sang before falling off a moving cloud blurred into a clatter of plods and no amount of poetic white noise can drown out the silence of years passed me by.

i am a hypocrite. talking of a dancing crowd when my back is breaking from the weight of dead butterflies rotting in my stomach. i write of blue skies when mine is auburn, polluted with the dust raised in my waking. the windows. the stars. the flowers. the steaming cup of coffee. the fragrances. and smouldering cigarettes. all lies. where is the acrid taste left in the crack of lips where i danced my tongue into a twist longing for the taste of nothingness? where is the death and falling of petals, the stain a years' rain imprinted on my dirty window? the sweat of words held beneath the swell of goose bumps. the coffee that ran cold in my hand but i drank it anyway, metallic and all. scratch that. i hate coffee. reminds me of a man i used to know. like a freshly brewed cup, he loved me with his tongue. i remember the rust in his voice, the bitterness on his breath. but i'd rather it hot. as it burns down my throat, i'm reminded in the reincarnation of wounds, masochist was a foreign trade i willed myself into learning.

somebody remind me, that love demands death of self.

and life became another wish-ingrained coin buried under a patch of brown earth in a field of grass that soon was raided by the green of indifference, i clicked my tongue in mourning, pursed my lips in silence and flashed the white of teeth in perceived happiness but in the confine of walls, it was a head buried beneath the fluff of pillows, eyes watering my nose into flight until my mouth was a host of slime.

no one taught me how to cry

my heart is an endless bonfire that won't put out in the falling of tears, i call jesus in the emptiness of my room, echoes ring with the smell of garlic and cigarettes i smoked last month that still burn at the bottom of my lungs.

he sees my yearning and asks me if i am deep. i wonder if my heart doesn't show in the breadth of my yawning

be still, he says to my gatherers' feet

i'm a nest builder

hands weighed down with loot
rolled up paper poems
a heart of another
dixie cups stained with brew
an overfilled ashtray

a light pours across my morning floor

and i drop it all
dust off a hallelujah from my night stand
melt down the scriptures iced between earwax

i fold my growing shadow into the bedroom corner

at noon, it's silver
and larging through the slits in my belief

i drop the expanse where he watches over me
 gather darkness into sacks like a pack rat

how possible is it
he still loves me

lint and void places

today i stood in the doorway
collecting rain in my hands
watching the drops pool
then trickle down in fingered rivulets

i re-enacted our days together,
rebuilt your scent on petrichor

i mourned over everything.
like the calculus i did in my head
to get the hospital-corners right
whenever you slept over

the lint missing from the sheets
that clung to your hair when you left
i walked through unsaid words
like wet paint walls
careful not to touch a syllable

then the rain stopped
the sky began to blue
and the air belched bird noises

i stood in the doorway
willing my eyes to weep

i felt nothing

tar threads up the walls where i walk

a rust of nails burrows fangs
into my chest like an army of fire ants
hooks skewering my brain to earlobes
lips to breast

tail stuffed up my scrambling mouth,
i wear the smile of a runaway sun
teeth and fangs tagging
a boulder of night clouds

in full hands
i gather moss off footprints
bottle the remnants of a slippery day
on a babble of blinds

through a hedge of whispers
a fluid morning slithers
in whooshes and sparks
like velcro shadows ripping off my skin
leaving a nylon rim of emptiness

bind my fingers to hold that old time grace

i'm leaden and brittle
seasoning a bland smile with alcohol

the scriptures mother read to me
i roll into blunts
they burn holes through my fingers

i round smoke rings
on cracked lips
they still won't make a halo

i search through my lungs for a fire
finding tar
in the voice of a boy
who called me hot

corrupted files
pile at the center of my emotions
an altar of insecurities

morphine numbness rapes my tongue
i won't yield a hallelujah

i'm a wicked man
mercy falls through my hands
like a tropical storm

i would take a double portion of communion
and still not feel clean

fix me jesus
before i drown inside my own wrists
bind my fingers together
to hold that old time grace

a draft drags unlaced shoes

through the clutter on my bedroom floor.

depression is the sound of its unrehearsed song

bare feet

i bet you thought you'd have it figured out by now. gravity.
the pulse of a wind. the architecture of webs. theology.
cathedral bell chimes. name it. twenty five and you're still
licking your lips to stop them from cracking. still biting your
nails. still mindlessly twisting your hair into knots. still raising
hell on loose slippers. your pillow still collecting lesser rain
falling off your face, never enough to water purpose or
meaning. darkness blurs the lines between your sheets.
dreams smoulder like blunts and are disposed off, ashen and
smoked out. a couple shots of tequila and you believe life is
perfectible only to wake up strewn across yet another
stranger's unmade bed. head spinning and there goes another
saturday. you stay up all night, sleep in all day. Another
monday. another week. month, year, another life not lived.
you still believe in shooting stars. and miracles. and a god
who loves you and will give you that longed-for 'quick fix' no
questions asked. or a god who will strike you down with
lightning and pump sense into your brainless head with
thunder. what is pure? what is true? should life be lived to fit
a fancy black suit? be spent wondering which shade of pale
accentuates the shape of one's closed-eye face? after all, isn't
that how we all go down or up in flames?

-take one

i'll forget the obscure for a while and talk about the day
passing outside my door. because some day, no one will
remember a blue faced girl bending over the edge of midnight

resuscitating a dying dream. outside my window, crickets giggle at shadows playing in a dimming moon. the big houses across are a procession of square orange lights that put out one after the other until the hill is a silhouette against a starry horizon. click by clack, i hear the noise turn in for the day until the air belches silence. and all life is lazy, rubbing a hand over its belly. trees reach out to pick stars, coming out with nothing but leaves in their hands. a breeze strokes her fingers through the grass, coming out without a song. everything reminds me of how weak i am. how i've walked these paths and come out with nothing but a film of dust on my heels.

i want to think of a perfect day. a symphony of raindrops. the communion of sunsets. an overfed child. hair that dances when the hills breath out. legs that don't tremble when asked to dance. i want to remember a baby on the bus. how when she flashed me a toothless grin i imagined the smile of god.

but i can't.

mon homme

i once knew a man who loved coffee
he'd swallow pints and smile

as they burned through his sore throat
swearing he saw visions of christ
in the static ascending to his mind peak

when he held me in his gaze, i soaked

in his infatuation for hot black things
mon homme
mon amour

i'd spread my hands at the burning end of his cigarette
to keep warm for him and for what? for
chrissake why?

i was ashen and ready to fall
when he fished in his pocket
for the next stick
before putting me out
with the sole of his shoe

you'd think i knew better
he never held me a woman
in the way his eyes wobbled over my rib cage
as if wondering if he'd catch disease
fucking me
or the way he sweated above me
like an archaeologist digging the earth
for fossils to validate his existence

i remember the way my legs fell apart
begging him to fuck all sin out of me
 i prayed to birth a child lighter

than the abomination i was doomed to exist as

in february i grew my nails out
to peel the stained skin off of me
but the deeper i ploughed into my thighs
the blacker scars became
and no amount of bleach
could dye my iodine face
no amount of rain could erode my dirt

i wore the mask of market products
a dab of pink on the cheeks
 wondering if he could tell the hurt
buried beneath the layers of hue

i held tears precious and still
on a decent day, they'd mirror the sky
you'd almost think me beautiful
in the blue of my eyes

i worshiped veet tubes to define my femininity
as plastic slabs voyaged up my legs
rip-ripping through my skin
woe was mine to behold
in the way he loved africa
to associate with suffering

only to deposit all his pained artefacts
at my wrists
with no return address

i'd take penitence
for knees that stutter before lesser gods
that egypt stretched to my father's courtyard
that i served him menstrual blood in a dixie cup
that i licked his ashtray lips
and carried his sin on my tongue
but i'll never apologize for loving someone
the colour of jesus
to birth a generation that won't curse themselves
to a six feet abyss that breathes
when a yellow moon roams the sky
asking me to bow, bow, bow to its dimmed throne

each night i sit in the dark
mouth fucking cholesterol and protein
i caress my growing belly
stroking the child of manic depression
hoping that maybe
        maybe
the yellow of my disease will
coat her skin
and her vernacular won't stutter
defining the voice of thunder

a testament of shadows

taut knees strum like violins
harmonizing the chorus of flies
coating my falling skin

i linger by the porch of a church
stroking a passing breeze
as if the robes of jesus

i walk through testament pages
fraying and browning the 4th gospel
on stained hands reaching
to touch the cross

i light candles
silhouettes reminding me
i am but a shadow upon a wall
a string of words
in the mouth of a poet

to walk or maybe crawl

she looked to the roof of the rock
beneath which she was caged
thinking
no way god could possibly fit in there
there just wasn't enough room
to fit his head
and the air smelled like smoke

she had learned how to tremble
in the thumping of rain
and the grumbling of knees
to shudder
in the quiver of fingers
fighting not to write suicide notes

she'd watch rain collect in puddles
then slip into the cracked earth
before baptizing her

she nursed at the breast of clouds
leaden and lifeless
when the sun passed by
in pride they'd say
this is my child
see her and weep

one day
god was taking a walk in the skies
when he heard muffled cries
from the cradle of clouds
"come out" he said

and she did

no one taught her to crawl
no one taught her to walk

we loved like rain

slow and incessant
like a drizzle
soaking our dirt

then all sudden
like a storm
eroding everything in our way

on petrichor, our liquid breaths rose
through the veins of deities
like incense of a burnt offering

like a weathered cliché

~ *i have found love to be commonplace, a reason why most seekers never find it.*

scars beckon a long gone youth

the sun wandered through split blinds and pooled on the tiles in yellow puddles, he looked like a man skating on banana peels as he roamed the room readying to go out. dark and square, he towered like a swiss flag. he bent down to kiss my forehead, aftershave spilling over my face. a thin breeze and a pool of sunshine. i suddenly felt not enough, kinky hair, polka pajamas and morning breath.

> beckoning night sky
> shield the scars of my gone youth
> before the sun come

the door clicked hesitantly. i heard his scent gently wander into the traffic. i started a poem about beautiful things, rain and dandelions. i painted the moon in black ink. silence wrapped herself in a blank page like a sleeve blanket angling flaccid arms not to look like a cliché. words suddenly felt not enough as despair wore a coat of noise ready to go out.

> resplendent noon sky
> cradle this crown of darkness
> before you are spent

between frets

i slide off the spittle of your hate
numb arms
wobbling in the intermittent rains
falling through your teeth
the pieces of silver
you hog inside the mouth that
once kissed me

you gaze into my eyes
like judas windows
i'm still balled in a corner
scraping bloodied nails over the walls
you built around me
white dust falls like
ghosts of manic pasts
dropping their bags below my eyes

i pull longing's shackle closer
like frayed woollen socks
too worn to leave welts

my cheeks are caked in mascara
darker than night
i count sheep by day
ways to die by night
still coming short
by you

i can hear it

the tap, tap, tapping
what's that sound-
tick, tick, ticking
hands on a wall
search, search, searching
for purpose
round and round
i'm spinning off wobbly feet
into white noise

but i'll still pretend there's music somewhere between these
frets

teasing the taste of a stranger's name on my tongue

his eyes fluttered in staccato as i reached for the lighter he
clutched in his hand like a penny about to conceive a wish, i
imagined that's how his heart flickered when i winced a
learned smile and lied to him about everything but the fact
that i wrote poetry, the blush in my cheeks fighting to get
used to a stranger's name.

> deceit recurred like
> adornment but no lie lay
> in the way we kissed

he smelled of vanilla and coffee arabica, he bounced his walk
like a spring day when he hugged me i felt disjointed from the
cloud of depression i carried around my neck. he told a tale
of thorns letting the blood set into blooms; i crept out of my
skin to smell the air.

> my feet soared yonder
> lingering on fevered brush
> where love wandered through

he loved rain in the way his eyelids wavered slightly shut to
the tapping of a drizzle on the roof and loved me in the silver
slits that kept me in sight when i pretended to look away.

> of all things i saw
> i want to remember love
> in unconscious stares

the twenty first hour

midday; and my bed is all hands and tongues
 i howl into the pillow
to scare off the scent of a beckoning blackness

static creeps over off-white walls
like tiny ants carving dynasties in my head

the wind since forgot to blow by
my room is heavy with a stench
of dreams stagnating at my doorstep

5pm; shadows lodge in my throat
solid and bitter; they threaten
to regurgitate every smile
i ever forced into my stomach

the twenty first hour collapses
upon my chest like d-cups
damned to a sagged existence

it stretches and twists
perks and falls;
then like a canine tongue
hangs and droops all over the rug
drowning any crumb of hope
that missed the nozzle
of a manic vacuum

glum countenance

i slither between slippery walls
in lethargic ups and downs
sorrow's tail stuffed in my mouth

the fluid gaze of could-have-been
since set into boulders
they roll through me
finding nothing to gather
in the moss shadows
sticking to my skin like velcro

i could have been a lover;
perhaps one who glories
in the richness of a morning sun
where days walk blind
in the footprints of runaway dreams

(but)

indifference holds a hammer to my emotions
where love came close
hands lingering
on the nip of my breast
but not deep enough to touch
the rim of my famished heart

lips tag brash whispers to my earlobe
the babble of believers
scrambling up my hedges
like an army of fire ants

burrowing
fangs and nails
into my chest
for all things synthetic
only coming out with tar
(but) never the tears bottled
in a smile full of teeth

each night i watch the dark
spark and crackle
like the nylon threads of thoughts
being ripped from my brain
on invisible hooks

reliquary (i)

i have no business desiring love

the holy grail of a homeless man
should be a roof
not the poetry of pallid rains

my fingers are smouldering
in yesterdays' fires
i can't shake the ashes
lest i put out

the wind of his wake winnowed
the substance of our encounter
leaving feathers in my burned-out hands

i have no business desiring love

but when a brown eyed boy
smells of wild flowers
and breakfast coffee
i dip my feathers in ink
and stick him between my pages
divine and precious
like a relic

reliquary (ii)

his eyes were neon lights
straitjacketing deception
in a spill of gold
i was a curious child
tracing the face of a lamp
with naked fingers

my skin thawed out
into a plush of hues
pouring face first
into his avid arms

he pulled the blinds
down my cheeks
writing himself saline
and jagged
in runoff mascara

i've still not learned a thing
i fold those inked sheets
where memory withers
like the wildflowers on his breath
into crisp ampersands
in wait for him
to finish me

reliquary (iii)

i bounce penknife metaphors
on clanking kneecaps
never high enough
to peg him to a cross

he still lies- cold
in an air
that already forgot his name. to me

another stoned memory
wedged beneath my lifeless shoes

the threshold

for Joy (RIP)

how do i recount your passing
on the panes of a window where
you stand whittling my fingers
on your crystal smile without

smudging blood all over these lines?

we met on a march day.
i remember the cold sinking
horizons into your asthma
i covered you with my red sweater
feeling the rhapsody in your chest;
the first love song i ever heard

and we'd curl up in my bunk bed
in the tin roof dormitory
matching our breaths to the patter of rain

it hasn't stopped raining
since your sun dimmed
i've slid through ordinary dreams
chasing your laughter
 in the sliver drops
dribbling down my window

it was february when your music died
i'm still building bridges between
our unwritten verses

my mouth quivers into foreign tongues
i imagine it's the language of the place you went to
the 'i love you's' i never quite verbalized

cover me inadequate

i.

they poke me
like feathers in a threadbare hat
they poke me

the prayers a goddamn immaculate woman
binges on like narcotics
    i tremble

ii.
days are breaking in places i cannot touch
towed away on rundown wagons
into the noise of the city
    who's got the keys

iii.
o mother, hold my religion while i invade these streets

your words are missals
heard from the porch of a church,
faded and warm,
you spoon-fed me
through toothless grins
under the papyrus-thatch shed

you never saw me a child of a lesser god
in squash mouthfuls
my stomach couldn't hold

i bloomed like wildflowers
in the forgotten fields of vanity
grasping on weary winds
a thing of beauty on the outskirts of sight

    but they'd find me
    and they'd pluck me

i'd pretend to hold water in their vase prisons
arcing for scanty sunlight in stained windows

iv.
o mother, hold my grace while i dig the soils for my roots

v.
to the boy who
    found me lacking;
    only a confidence of a shadow
    a grey silhouette off black and white walls

the thought i still hold is your flared nostrils breathing me in.
i always thought if i looked close enough i'd see your heart
beyond those tonsils. one december night, they grew so large
from the cold. it was the night you said you loved me.
perhaps because i was the only thing that hadn't died. i
remember each syllable landing like a hammer nailing me to
the roof of your mouth.

    cover me inadequate
all the poems i wrote you into
were a vomit of stolen words
my stomach couldn't hold

vi.

to the boy who

    walked muddy feet into my torment
    called me sweet chocolate
    and set me on fire
    as though i was only worth
    molten and face up
    on the bed of his tongue

i remember reaching beneath your ears for pennies and
coming up with the brown of my bare palm. i filled
the pocket of your indifference with tears to make my own
fountains. shooting stars were shrouded in the cloud of your
hesitation, i wrote your name between candles just so i had
something to wish upon

to the boy whose stare dug too deep into my nails
the boy whose head my poetry held a gun to
to the almost lover,
the boy whose name i recite on the beads of a rosary of
narcotics

vii.

o mother, show me how to reach blistered feet across the
threshold of a church
i hear it clear now;
the grace between page 26 and 27 of the missal

the brass choir and
the violin solo rising, shadowing
    my inner screams
    rising, blurring-
    my unsung hymn
    rising, into the noise of the city
    who's got the keys

beneath the sepia skirts of twilight

one would say kampala is a heaving laggard entity
her fluffy red tail of rear-lights
drags over potholed tarmac
 leaving wisps of dust in its wake

smoke crawls out of her exhaust
fusing into the brawny air
chock-full on rollup cigarettes
fake coffee and low-priced cologne

harried footsteps
scour through weeds spotting the city like acne
as silence bleeds in deliberate trickles
into pavement cracks
levitating a staleness of decomposing leaves
and other things forgotten

one would say the city is a cold stuttering thing
that gapes into the void beyond traffic light poles
away from soiled fingers knocking her window down
for a cent, she wheezes up a whirlwind on green

twilight illuminates gaps between buildings
wrapping sepia robes over grey walls
sipping through dirt-stained glass
with obstinate poise
warming taciturn apartments with mellow embrace

often, kampala is a scenic zingy city
cooling in lethargic ticks and tocks
folding away on crackly chalk knuckles

convex tree figures slow dance in a lazy draft
silhouetting against dimming sidewalks

run-down cars groan and grumble
waning into discreet suburban nights
where the city goes to snooze

but we are not ready to go home
we lace our shoes with blitzed strings of midnight
till dawn sways into the city in golden stilettos

fugitive

i met you in a tropical town
blue eyes, auburn hair
alien and glorious
like spring bloom
you dyed my poetry

in fugitive colour
    this is beautiful, you said
    and let it linger

i once knew the taste of dust,
pepper and burnt earth
you tasted of cigarettes
and insatiable want
    you're sweet, you said
    and let it devour

you corrupted my skin with your stubble
i forgot how to feel but the heat on your tongue
melting goose bumps on my ice chest
i might love you, i said
    isn't that something, you said
    and let it burn

i wrote you into poetry a wrecker's ball
knocking down the walls of my tear ducts
i still clang to your knees like a penitent
tacking loose tears into my braids
    i do (love you), you lied
    and let it sting

you airlifted on silence
as if afraid i'd trace you by your footprints
i searched night skies for incense
only discovering madness in off-white crescent moons
blinking stars and water
and wind and all things red
anything that reminded me of you
insanity weaved itself into my sheets
    i let it make a bed

just as easily as you had thrust the blade
just as fast as you had signed me off to die

i met him in a tropical town
damaged and wounded as i was
wringing bloodied hands
    i love a woman of war, he said
    and let me forget you

burning down altars with your lighters

two lighters, a packet of cigarettes and a train wreck

i held the stuff you left behind like relics
stick onto stick, building arks of smoke
'til my fingers were soldering into ashes
i couldn't blow away to sea
lest it sailed me back to you

i remember the sky plunging into me

with cloudy vengeance
where god forgot me
like the dominion cocking his gun on israel's head

i remember
constructing pyramids on your memories
chanting your name on g major
'til i was out of breath

i burned altars of emotion with
your lighters
invoking you with liquid sacrifices
i ran out of waterworks

looking back at the war in my knees
when your eyes torched my legs
i was never righteous enough to deify you

looking at this cloudless sky where
your rains ceased to fall
your eyes were never a thing to drown in

concrete scratches the wounds on her knees like therapy

her younger father lifts a leg
to water a roadside shrub,
with gibber reeling off his torn
lips

grandma warms frail lungs on a
wooden pipe
her brother's on the news
in carrot yellow

her sister pops pills and laughs-
she got the prescription wrong

but mother is loudest;
on her knees mouthing
silent creeds

with seven candles i invoke you

i.
i get furnished remembering wednesday.
i met you in a suburban café with chalk-painted walls
resonating in the inexorable pop of a rhumba
your red hair floated on a twirl
where you bent whispering in slurred accents
it's sad to imagine you noticed my vile face
when your eyes twinkled unearthly shades
off disco lights
    'pardon me'
you leaned closer
your breath heating my earlobe
like a cigarette ready to burn
my mind flooded with fire
i was a brittle bush in july

ii.
here's the thing about love
thursday lifts her twilight robes
a gaze at her star-filled thighs
you swear you've seen the face of god

your knees tremble
pleading sanction
your belly rumbles
with wrecked rhapsodies

in that moment
you're unafraid of being late to work the next day
in that moment
you're not afraid of deposition

iii.
your sultry hands pulsed into me
heedless of season
stroking my clock face
till i was spinning
-whirling-
sunday was a thing with wings

iv.
you were an ethereal being
i drank in sangria mouthfuls
letting you sit on my tongue
'til my lips were red
i imagined that's what your heart
looked like beating through friday evenings
like a deadline

the sun wielded vermilion pompoms
raising dust to the roof of your mouth
you choked out tarred accolades
    'how beautiful you are!'
i ingested them in insatiable bites
side- stepping your allusions to cocoa yens

v.
(saturday) tell me i'm not alone in this sin

vi.
(your body was an effing deceit)

your sand paper cheeks scraped my skin
where you crawled through my heart
rolling my emotions into cigarette paper

you ignited me with the flames in your eyes
inhaled me like smoke
and spat me out in hasty fits
like an abomination

you faded into liquid skies
leaving me grey with static

i remember tuesday like an abrasion

vii.
i am not asking the heavens to regurgitate rain
just so i don't get wet
i am not asking trains to derail if the tracks
don't windup in your heart
i am not asking mondays not to be blue
just so your eyes take the prize
i am not asking you to pull down the sun
and gift it to me by night
i am only asking your arms to turn around and love me

in the doorway

i am become an underdone egg
rocking back and forth in a rusty brown keg
questioning why i feed this beast
with blood off my wrist

my sheets are a thousand thorns
pin-pricking me with tons of scorn
a certain death garbed in pale skin
pinning me down, adjudicating my sin

on the outskirts of well wasted time
i feel alive and in my prime
nothing out there can hold me back
in my life, reeling up the slack

momma says she birthed me with a spoon
i sip off a fountain, this is my high noon
i burn dejection on the end of a cigarette
toe-wrenching rue, i won't give a sweat

in the doorway, flakes stand arms akimbo
clogging my exit with gibberish lingo
i shoot through the roof like a stray bullet
you can't stop me, i am become volcanic summit

on the outskirts of well wasted time
i feel alive and in my prime
nothing out there can hold me back in my
life, reeling up the slack

tell the snooze button to take a hike
i'll catch a sunrise, what's not to like
nothing out there can hold me back
in my life, reeling up the slack

muse is samsara

at six
i wrote my first poem
at least that's what mum calls
the marinated bookmark lodged between
the pages of her then-workbook

it read
daddy bought a shiny blue pickup
with a band trapped inside the dashboard
daddy is so rich
we have ten fans in our house

honestly
the village wasn't electrified
and i first saw a real-life fan at twelve
but our house did have two doors and eight large windows
muse was a giggly little girl with loose braids in a draft

at fourteen, i met a pompous sixteen year old
with sticks up his (pitch-black place)
he marched fire-ant feet into my lungs
gobbled up all of my oxygen

muse sat in a tiny compartment
rocking thin arms back and forth
like a deranged woman
begging him to look up into my face
      he didn't
muse collected dust from a shackle on his bedpost

twenty: i took to the bottle
beat the bejesus out of muse
demanding a confession
she took blades to her wrists
bled into fluffy things

diaries crammed the bookshelf like a garage sale

twenty five
muse is a gatherer

she is a child
swallowing melon seeds
to grow orchards
in her chest region

she is sodden brokenness
trapping raindrops in dreary palms
an inebriated prayer on the back of a runoff
she's a nosy neighbour documenting
other people's misery while depression
nudges a trigger by my mouth
she's a suicide note, she's a resurrection

she's samsara

it might be your luck and war will find you

you hide beneath vehement shadows of wrecked disposition
midst brittle corpses
solemnly swearing they look like you

you gnaw on cardboard wishes
that love might rescue you before
one insatiable grave says it's your turn

that funeral procession of fleas
lapping on your liquid brain
your feet want to wheel across the room
-away-
into silk drapes dancing alone in the twilight

but men are such brutes
they woo and feed you on throaty deceptions

you know you're no cute little thing

still, you wear those white lies l
ike a bridal veil
and march out of the webbed vestry
to a band of broomsticks striking cymbaled floors
strings strum-strumming, but aren't violins

you will know war found you while you sought love

hope is a luxury i can't afford (oprihory)

how do i swear off polar meds
when i keep writing blunt-edged words
into my skin for the jolt
as they strain their way out of my chest cavity
poking leftover bruises with renewed enthusiasm
of countless feet i let into my holiest places
pilgrimaging back to their quieter existences

how do i define the life of me
when hope is an elixir i cannot afford to borrow-
another repressed shadow caught in the webs beneath my
bed;
a house my demons abandoned when they moved into my
brain
leaving their bags by the porch of my eyes

raging despair starts fires on cigarette breaks
but troubles that come to bed with me
are ice cubes between soot-stained walls
crack-cracking
saturating my dementia
liquefying- they still won't baptize me

nights became haunted
sheep don't matter anymore
i count ways to die
but how shall i go when
the words left inside of me
aren't enough to complete a suicide note

note to suicide:
you are a six feet
square faced temptation
that's way out of my league you can
walk into my poetry
anytime you please as long you
promise to keep out of mother's searching eye

dear mother:
of all the things i picked from you
square teeth and extravagant eyes
i should have clasped the
mumble of don'ts
you waged at me on my twenty fifth birthday
but you never ceased to remind me
i had my father's legs so i raced
away from your onrushing squalls

dear squall:
you found me anyway, didn't you
in his sand coloured arms
that derailed me
off a manic spin

of all the things i still remember
through gunfights and white noise
he carried whispers on the podium
of his tongue
when he made whistle-stop tours
of my ruined cities

dear city:
your pale walls
remind me of his skin
on which i was only a silhouette
dark as sin

your colossal sky scrapers
remind me how invisible i am
how can god possibly see me from his window

i'm stuck in a dust filled closet
where he hangs me
as a trophy
not bright enough to light
his bed rest

dear rest: one day, i'll find you

dear you:
here i go letting you take something else that's mine
(again! i should have listened to mother)
kindly let yourself out of my poems
and slam the door after you

this was supposed to be crisp and petite
but i'm done being boxed up
in the callous cages of critics
my life is not a pile of clever metaphors
folded into funky shapes to look pretty
like dinner table napkins

dear napkin:
come here you
only you can deal all of my tears
without scraping a heart

dear heart:
i need you to not be in on this

crayons

a yellow girl in a camouflage scarf-
she sits next to me taking notes

on blue cardboard.
from the podium
the voice of reason speaks
'first, second, third generation-
we are one.
children and immigrants,
this is our home'
she picks her whitewash
and sketches seventeen heads-
seventeen chalk faces
green eyes and pouty pink mouths.
she then takes a pencil
and draws the eighteenth face
me, fading into the damn cardboard

the moon knelt
lapping at a rusty puddle

i drew nigh
when she switched knees

praying her muddied metaphors

sprinkle over my blank skin

he drags his red mud boots over my black and white dream

this could be us

your level smile negotiates my suggestive curves
arcing your brown eyes
into twinkled narrow streets
liquid heat evanesces resolve
inviting/ begging/ demanding

i tally heartbeats on jelly fingers
trying to stay sane is too much
i reach for your chiseled chin
for the twitch in your cheek
your stubble scribbles jumbled oaths

on my forehead -staccato gasps
baptize me
hands reading goose bumps like braille
possess me
my insides play ragtime rhythms

unconscious prayers strewn all over my body
it glistens like a medieval cathedral
you embrace me like communion

you cradle me like i might break
you cradle me like it's gonna hurt

then you're gone
your red mud boots sinking

into the edge of a waning moon
your finest work -these red blushed cheeks
flung into obscure captions

grey walls, grey roof, me
just an extra in a black and white puzzle
you detoured into

/sniff/
bits of you fall out of my soggy eyes
but it will take exorcism to get over you

i'm a thinly marinated pickle

only an agnostic blur

to a hunger eye

…not enough

dear nothingness (oprihory)

again, i'm on purple knees wheezing through the
slime building up beneath my tongue as rage pulls at
my braids asking me to suck harder, faster, harder... i was
taught to shut my mouth- be a lady, i stacked hellos and cuss-
words between clenched teeth my mouth stunk like the pen
of a poet, (i swear) the green on my gasp could make a city
weep.

note to a city that weeps: your plucked eyebrows and coffee
breaths and stilettos forever rushing through deadlines
remind me of a man i used to know, bitter and loud like a
soliloquy swinging dusty feet off a wooden bar-stool at noon.
i've learned to live in your shadow if i am ever to write the
journeying sun into my poetry but for tonight, i'm sorry you'll
have to get in line and shut the fuck up while i bleed

note to bleeding: my body was always open for your monthly
visits but you overstayed your welcome with the crimson
soap messages you signed on the mirror of my verse.

dear verse: i was told god walks somewhere between your
breaks but my pages read of stressed words that don't rhyme,
so please stop wasting my time

dear time: wrap up your tired song
walk that ticking cliché out of my head

note to cliché: you're the reason i'm still lonely. the poet runs from you yet i find myself drawn to the innocence of your love.

dear love: why do i even bother? you're still that skinny bitch with perfect skin that's way out of my league, i'm your ugly best friend carrying your expensive baggage on a smile full of braces while you wave a manicured hand to nothingness.

dear nothingness: i could check a thesaurus for a prettier word but what difference would it make putting a pink bow in your hair and glass sandals upon your feet, you will always be just that, nothing, yet, i'm still dragged into your scentless fragrance

dear fragrance: you remind me of french indifference and the red head from Bordeaux who smoked too many cigarettes his teeth were the yellow of a night lamp i mothed up to, only for him to turn off.

dear off: i could use some of you right now

ABOUT THE AUTHOR

Faith lives and writes in Uganda. Her work has appeared in poetry anthologies such as *"imagine. ex-plore. create. inspire."* and *"the alphabet soup poetry anthology"*. She has also been featured on literary websites, like Tangled Routes, allpoetry.com and The Blue Nib magazine.

www.ingramcontent.com/pod-product-compliance
Lightning Source LLC
Chambersburg PA
CBHW070104070426
42448CB00038B/1503